W9-ARV-881

Table of Contents

Photo Credits: Cats

R.E. Barber: pages 11, 16, 19
Erwin & Peggy Bauer: pages 10, 12, 14-16, 18, 20, 21, 24, 25, 27, 28
Norvia Behling: pages 12, 28
Tony La Gruth: page 22
James Martin: pages 24, 29
Laura Riley: pages 11, 14
Kevin Schafer: pages 22, 26, 27, 30
Fred Siskind: page 31
Rita Summers: pages 8, 10, 16, 24
Charles Summers: pages 15, 18
Robert Winslow: 8, 12, 13, 15, 24, 25
Animals Animals/Samburu G.R.: page 17
Animals Animals/Gerard Lacz: page 27
Tim Davis/Davis-Lynn Photography: pages 8, 9, 13, 16, 18, 22, 23, 26
Renee Lynn/Davis-Lynn Photography: pages 8-10, 15, 16, 18-20
John Giustina/Wildlife Collection: pages 11, 20, 30
Martin Harvey/Wildlife Collection: pages 10, 14, 16
Dean Lee/Wildlife Collection: page 19
Vivek R. Sinha/Wildlife Collection: page 31

Front Cover: center - Animals Animals/Peter Weimann;
upper left - Martin Harvey/Wildlife Collection; upper right - Davis/Lynn Images
End Pages: front -Davis/Lynn Images; back - Ellis Nature Photography

CATS

WHAT IS A CAT ?

Domestic
Burmese
kitten

There are about three dozen different species of cats, all in the family Felidae. They are diverse in size, from a ten-foot, 600-pound tiger, to the smallest domestic house cat weighing only a few pounds. But all cats (felines) share many of the same characteristics.

Cats are grouped into categories: big cats—the lion, tiger, leopard, and jaguar; and small cats, which include cats in the full range of sizes. The difference between the two is not size but sound—the big cats can roar, the small cannot.

POUNCING PREDATOR

Jaguar

The cat is a jumping, leaping creature able to land on its feet and pinpoint its landing. With lightning quick reflexes, agility, and strength, cats balance in risky places, recover from falls, and spring off the ground. As a leaping, pouncing predator the jaguar is deadly accurate.

COATS OF COLOR

The colors and markings of the cat are its glory. Every coat is individual. The black stripes of the tiger are his own. The spots of the cheetah, leopard, and jaguar are all different. Most coats match their surroundings so that the stealthy, hunting cat will not be heard *or* seen.

Cheetah

NAME THAT CAT

Cats have wonderful names like jaguar, puma, ocelot, cheetah, and lynx. Many of the names were given by people who respected and feared the fierce cats that lived among them. Jaguar comes from the South American Indian name *yaguara*, which means "a beast that kills its prey with one bound."

Cougar

African
wild cat

8

Bengal tiger

THE BEAUTIFUL BEAST

All cats are carnivores, meat-eaters who hunt for their food. Their bodies are like well-oiled machines with flexible skeletons, strong muscles, excellent eyesight, keen hearing, powerful jaws, and vicious teeth. They are the nearest thing to a perfect stalking, hunting animal in the world. Because of their beauty, secretiveness, and fierceness, cats have always been a symbol of mystery and power to man.

Domestic longhaired calico

HOUSE CAT HISTORY

The sociable domestic cat is the favorite pet of millions of people. Descended from the African wild cat, cats began living with humans in Egypt about 4,000 years ago. They were so valued that the Egyptians considered them sacred and worshipped them in the form of a goddess that had the head of a cat.

The marvel of the house cat is its double nature. A delightful, tame companion, the cat still has the body of a hunter and carries a touch of the wild wherever it lives.

FELINE FEATURES

The physical ways of cats are fascinating. No one trait in itself, but a combination of characteristics, enables cats to feed, communicate, and live successfully in many different habitats.

UNDERCOVER ▲

A cat is a warm-blooded animal with a double-layered fur coat that protects it from wet and cold. The outer layer is made up of long, coarse hairs called guard hairs. The under fur, close to the body, is soft and downy,

The thick fur of these two snow leopards enables them to live on the cold Himalayan mountains of Asia.

CLEAN MACHINE

Cats groom or clean themselves, and each other, with a built-in scrub brush, a tongue rough as sandpaper. A cat's tongue is covered with tiny, hard spikes—perfect for picking up loose dirt or hair, or rasping the last shreds of meat off a bone.

SLEEPY HEAD

Catnap is a word invented to describe the way cats sleep—for short periods of time. This ocelot, like all cats, sleeps *often*—about twice as much as other animals.

EAR FULL

Cats, masters of silence in their own movements, are quick to hear the noises that others make. With funnel shaped outer ears and a keen sense of hearing, cats can pick up sounds that are too faint or too high for humans to hear.

10   African caracal

TOUGH TALK ▲

Cats have their own communication system: hissing, spitting, growling, and snarling. Purring, the perfect sound of contentment, is for pleasure.

WHISKER WAYS ▶

A cat's whiskers are not just cute. They are organs of touch almost as sensitive as fingertips. They help a cat avoid objects, judge spaces, and feel its way in the dark.

◀ MINE!

A cat is a territorial creature. It will scratch trees and spray urine to mark its property, so that other cats will keep off. A domestic cat has more civilized ways of marking. It may rub the furniture or a person's legs with the scent glands on its head or at the base of its tail.

11

BUILT
TO KILL

To be a cat is to be a hunter. It has been said that every cat is a beast of prey, even the tame ones. And so it is. The house cat who eats from a bowl or stalks birds in the backyard and the mountain lion who bites through the neck of a deer, have the same instincts. Their physical structure makes them excellent killers.

A natural climber, the mountain lion can spring straight up as high as 18 feet, or drop down 60 feet without getting injured.

UNDERCOVER CATS

Most wild cats that live in dense [gra]ss, brush, or jungle have coats [tha]t blend with their surroundings. [Da]ppled, spotted, or striped, a cat's [coa]t can make it nearly invisible. [No]w you see it now you don't— [the] undercover hunter.

[SN]EAK [AT]TACK

[A]ll good hunters are sneaks, [an]d cats are the sneakiest. [Str]ong muscles allow a cat to [stal]k and hide, then surprise its [pr]ey. With enormous muscle [co]ntrol, this Canadian lynx [mo]ves ever so slowly towards its [vic]tim, then freezes. A cat can [sta]y motionless for half an hour [or] more—and then pounce on its [star]tled prey.

[THE] EYES HAVE IT

[A] cat's eyes are deadly [hu]nting weapons. Their [nig]ht vision is amazing— [six] times greater than that [of] humans. In the dark, [the] pupils of a cat's eyes [ex]pand to take in more [ligh]t. These pupils, nearly [filli]ng the eyes, are strange [and] beautiful. But beauty [is n]ot the point. Detecting [pre]y is the purpose.

FLEXIBLE FELINES

A cat's spine is so flexible that it can twist and turn and bound at its prey from any angle. This lioness is stretching after having rested most of the day.

CAT DRACULA

Canine teeth are for killing, and a cat's got the best. Cats use their four dagger-like canine teeth to bite the back of an animal's neck. Nerves at the base of these teeth guide them between the vertebrae (spine bones) of their prey. The bite is so accurate that it cuts the spinal cord *between* the bones and the victim dies instantly.

PAW CLAWS

Claws are a cat's secret weapon. Most of the time a cat's claws stay inside its paws. During an attack, a cat automatically whips out the claws like razor-edged knives. Afterward, the claws retract to a relaxed position inside the paws. The cat returns to its silent walk, but the claws are always ready.

The outstretched claws of this kitten help it to hang on.

13

THE LITTLEST CATS

Care to cuddle a lion cub? Is there anything cuter than a kitten? Cats, wild and tame, give birth and care for their offspring in much the same ways. Except for lions, which live in groups, all young cats are cared for by their mother alone. In the wild, cubs lead a dangerous life and must learn to hunt and fend for themselves before leading independent lives.

Lioness and cubs

HOME BODIES▲

All cats are born blind and helpless and feed only on milk for six to eight weeks. But a young cat grows quickly and, in just a week, may double its body weight. A small cat may be on its own in a few months. But the large cats, like the lion and tiger, mature more slowly, and the cubs may depend on their mother for about two years.

AT HOME AND ON THE RANGE

To feed her cubs, a mother cat has to kill at least three times as much prey as when she lives alone. Smaller cats, like this bobcat, bring rodents and other prey back to the den. Larger cats may take their youngsters along and have them practice their hunting skills.

Clouded leopard cub

PLAYING TO KILL▼

Fighting with each other and stalking small animals for fun are the ways young cats learn to hunt on their own. What is playing today is hunting tomorrow. These snow leopard cubs are learning the survival skills they'll need as adults.

GETTING A GRIP

Children may claim that their parents are a pain in the neck, but not cats. Domestic and wild cats carry their young by the back of the neck—with no pain at all. Loose folds of skin on a kitten's neck are a natural handle. But the lion cub (above, left) would rather hitch a ride on its mother's back.

This young cheetah is learning, but the unharmed antelope is evidence that the cheetah needs more practice.

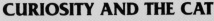

Lynx kitten

CURIOSITY AND THE CAT

All cats are curious, but kittens and cubs are especially anxious to explore their surroundings. Curiosity, however, sometimes gets cats into trouble. This lynx kitten now has to figure out a way to get down.

15

LEOPARD

CAT UP A TREE

The leopard is the smallest of the big cats, with an average weight of only 100 pounds. A compact powerhouse, the leopard is the master of surprise attack. The most graceful and sure-footed of all cats, the leopard is the best tree-climber. Secretive and rarely seen, a leopard can sometimes be spotted by its long, elegant tail dangling from a tree.

LETHAL LEAP

How does a leopard hunt? Patiently and silently. The leopard slinks. It creeps. It belly-crawls ever so carefully towards its prey. Then it *strikes* with a lightning fast leap—graceful, precise, and deadly.

TREETOP DINING

A leopard does not invite guests to dinner. In fact, it often drags its kill up a tree to keep it safe. A leopard can climb a tree with a carcass weighing more than 50 pounds clamped in its jaws. The cat stows the victim over a branch then takes a good rest knowing that its next meal is close by.

DIFFERENT AND THE SAME

A "black panther" is actually a leopard with a coat of almost invisible black spots on a black background. This beautiful dark cat has a savage reputation. But he is no different from other leopards than a blue-eyed person is from a brown-eyed friend.

THE SOUND OF SILENCE

Do not listen for a leopard. There is not much to hear. The noises a leopard makes are described as a growl or hiss, a rasping yowl or even a cough. It does not roar. Silence seems to suit the leopard best.

POOKY

The snow leopard [loo]ks like the ghost of a [leo]pard. Its thick, woolly [coa]t is a ghostly gray [wit]h black spots, well [suit]ed for its snowy habi-[tat]—the highest, coldest [mou]ntains in the world.

17

LIONS

LITTLE LIONS

One to five cubs are born in a lion litter, and they depend on their mother for almost two years. Their playtime is their schooltime. They "stalk" each other and "attack" one another, learning the hunting techniques they must know. When they've grown, the females remain at home, but the males are on their own. They set out to search for their own pride.

A MATTER OF PRIDE ▲

Lions are the only cats that live in groups, called "prides." As many as 40 cats can live in a pride — several lionesses, their cubs and 1 to 4 adult males. They all live together in a distinct territory, which can extend as far as 10 miles in any direction. The lionesses, who are usually all related, inherit the home range, so they must be especially proud of their pride.

GRRRR!

A lion's roar is so powerful that it can carry for 5 miles. The great GRRR! is an awesome sound, vibrating like thunder over the plains. Lions roar to stake out their neighborhoods, to let everyone know that the territory is theirs. Their roar is like a huge sign: Keep Off! No Trespassing! Or Else!

HUNT CLUB

Lions are the only cats that hunt as a group. They spot prey at a distance and set out with a plan. Surrounding an animal, they drive it toward hidden members waiting to attack. Because they work in groups, lionesses, who do most of the hunting, can easily bring down a wildebeest or zebra and even tackle a giraffe or young elephant—big game even for a big cat.

HUNGRY AS A LION ▼

Lions are not fussy eaters. They eat what they kill, what other predators kill, or animals that just die. And they have no table manners. They snarl and snap at each other, hogging their own portion. They gorge, rather than eat every day. In a single meal, a male lion may eat 80 pounds of meat—and then not eat for a week.

THE KING . . . AND QUEEN . . . OF BEASTS

The lion is known as the King of Beasts for good reason. A male lion can weigh as much as 500 pounds. The female is no less royal at 300. The male, with his magnificent mane, has the look of a monarch. He protects the pride and defends the females against intruders.

SLEEPY HEAD

Lions hunt and eat and. . . sleep. Mostly sleep. It has been said that lions are the laziest animals in Africa. If they've had a good hunt and their bellies are full, lions can spend 18 to 20 hours a day resting or sleeping in the shade.

19

NUMBER ONE RUNNER

The cheetah is the fastest land animal on earth, for short distances. It streaks across the plains at 70 miles an hour. The cheetah's most important hunting weapon is its amazing, deadly sprint. The cheetah runs for its supper and runs for its life.

▼ FUNNY FACE

Cheetah cubs are covered with a strange, pale gray fur on their head and back for the first few months. Their faces are funny, too. A cheetah's face is set off by 2 black stripes running from the inner corner of each eye to the mouth. On babies, these lines form an unhappy frown, making cheetah cubs the ugly ducklings of the cat world.

20

THE ONE AND ONLY

Cheetahs are so unlike other cats that they are a separate species. The claws do not retract. They do not have powerful jaws. Their canine teeth are not ferocious. They are not strong enough to drag their prey. They cannot roar or climb trees. They do not have long whiskers. They *do* have a deep chest filled with large lungs, and a slender, well-muscled body, built for speed.

ROYAL ROBES ▶

The king cheetah wears a royal coat different from the common cheetah. Rare and beautiful, the king has spots that blend into stripes down his back. Having stripes *and* spots makes him a kingly cat indeed.

SPEEDING TO KILL

Faster than a sports car, the cheetah bursts from zero to 40 miles per hour in two seconds. Its claws grip the earth like cleats. Its feet fly, hitting the ground so that, at times, all four feet are airborne. Still running, the cheetah knocks its victim flat, then pounces to kill.

SPRINGY SPINE

The secret to the cheetah's speed is its amazingly flexible spine. When running, the cat arches its back and pulls its feet together. Then, like a spring, its spine uncoils and its legs shoot out, giving the cheetah the longest stride in the cat world.

21

TIGERS

AWESOME CAT

Mystery, courage, fierceness—these are the characteristics of the biggest cat of them all, the tiger. Seven types of tigers roam various parts of Asia. The largest is the Siberian tiger, which can be more than ten feet long and weigh more than 600 pounds. Rarely seen, the tiger hunts alone at night, a silent, powerful creature, beautiful and frightening.

TIGER TOTS

Tiger cubs are born into a world that can be very hard. They may be killed by other animals while their mother is hunting. At 18 months to two years old, they leave their mother to find their own territory. There they will spend most of their life, hunting and living alone.

BEATING THE HEAT

It's hot in the jungle—steamy and sticky. A tiger can't take its fur coat off, but it can *swim*. Among big cats, the tiger is the most likely to cool off in the water.

Splashing, swimming, lounging up to its neck in lakes and rivers, the tiger knows how to get relief from the heat.

TELLTALE STRIPES

People have fingerprints; tigers have stripes. Every tiger has its own pattern of stripes. Tigers' faces are fierce and beautiful, but they are also unique. A tiger's face markings are so distinctive that they can be used to tell two tigers apart.

SHADOWY FIGURES

The tiger's magnificent striped orange-and-black coat is not just decoration. Stripes are the perfect camouflage in tall grasses and forests, where strips of light filter to the ground through dense leaves. Tigers that live in the northern climates are lighter in color to help them hide in the snow.

PALE FACE

A "white" tiger is not a ghost. It is a genuine tiger with a pink nose and charcoal-colored stripes on a white background. Its eyes may be blue—a tiger of a different hue!

THE STEALTH ATTACK

A tiger is not a hunter that chases prey. It creeps up under cover and gets as close as possible. Then it takes a great leap at the victim and strikes with a lethal weapon—the largest canine teeth of any meat-eating land animal. Still, hunting is not easy. Tigers catch only about one out of every 20 animals they go after.

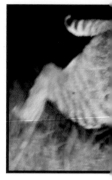

COUGAR, LYNX, AND BOBCAT

CATS HOT AND COOL

The cougar, lynx, and bobcat are most commonly found in northern climates, but these cats go their separate ways. The lynx is a creature of the snowbound woods. The bobcat prowls most of North America. But the cougar, also known as the puma, the panther, or the mountain lion, is a cat for all climates. It can be found on cold, high peaks, in steaming jungles, in swamplands, and even in deserts.

TUNED IN

A cat with antennae? The lynx has long, glossy, black "tufts" that stick up from each ear. Like hearing aids, they increase the cat's ability to detect the slightest sound. No creak, or snap, or thump in the forest gets by the listening lynx.

▲ DISAPPEARING SPOTS

Adult cougars have sleek, tawny coats that match their spooky yellow eyes. But cougar cubs are spotted with black. At six months, they begin to lose their spots and become cats of one color.

◀ This Canadian lynx is marking the pine tree with his scent.

◄ A CAT CALLED BOB

A stubby six-inch tail gives the bobcat its name. (To "bob" a tail means to cut it short.) Not a big animal all around, the bobcat weighs about 20 pounds and looks very much like its cousin the lynx.

PHANTOM OF THE FOREST

Bobcats hang out. These cats have favorite places—ledges, tree limbs, and trails—that they come back to again and again. Finding one of these sites may be the only way to lay eyes on a bobcat. These quick-as-a-wink cats are usually seen as fast flashes of fur in the forest.

RACING FOR RABBIT

For mountain cats that live in snow country, the snowshoe hare is a main meal. A swift runner on the biggest rabbit feet around, this hare is still no match for a hungry cat.

KILLER COUGAR

A large male cougar is 200 pounds of muscle. A fierce predator, he can kill a deer with one powerful bite. In his territory, no other animal can challenge him—except a barking dog. The yapping of a poodle sends a cougar up a tree.

CATS WITH A SOUTHERN ACCENT

Cats in Central and South America all test the limits of some feline characteristic. The jaguar has incredible power; the ocelot, extraordinary beauty. The jaguarundi is the most un-catlike creature, and the margay is a gymnast that does tricks in tree tops.

SPOTTED BEAUTY

The ocelot has a coat of many colors. Its background fur runs from reddish brown to cream to white. And its spots are a varied lot: solids, circles, and spots that join together to form stripes. The result is a masterpiece of camouflage and one of the most magnificent coats in the cat world.

A hungry jaguar on the prowl.

Margay

CIRCUS CAT
The margay is a trapeze artist, and its high wire is a tree branch. No bigger than a house cat, the margay scampers round trees like a monkey. An acrobat with special equipment, this cat as ankles that rotate way out and big feet and toes designed for gripping.

Jaguarundi

CAT COUPLES
The jaguarundi looks more like a weasel than a cat. It has a long body with legs that seem too short and a head that appears too small. But the jaguarundi male and female find each other attractive and, unlike most other cats, they live together for long periods of time.

27

ONE FIERCE CAT
Alligators and turtles beware! And monkeys, too! The jaguar plunges into rivers and scrambles up trees to feed its appetite. It dives, it swims, it leaps tall trees with a single bound. When this meat-eater is hungry, no one is safe!

WEATHERMAN
The jaguar is at home just about everywhere — mountains, grasslands, and rain forests. Everywhere it goes, the jaguar proclaims its presence with a roar that makes mountains tremble, grasses shiver, and jungles quiver. Amazon Indians still believe that the roar of the jaguar is the sound of thunder that announces approaching rain.

UNCOMMON CATS

Cats are exotic creatures, magnificent and mysterious, but also strange, and even bizarre. The cat kingdom has some surprising, remarkable, and fascinating felines.

BARE BODY ▶

The sphynx is a domestic cat, and no wonder. Without a hair on its body, it *must* live indoors. It would be hard to survive in the wild without a fur coat.

MOST WANTED

Geoffrey's cat has a distinction no other cat wants. Its fur is the most traded pelt in the world. Prized for its beauty, its exotic coat has black spots and colors ranging from smokey-gray to tawny yellow.

◀ RABBIT EARS

The serval has big ears that look more like they belong on a rabbit than a cat. But these ears serve the serval well. It can hear small animals hidden in grasses and pounce as quick as a . . . rabbit.

◀ SLAM DUNK

The caracal can leap into the air and swat a bird to the ground like a basketball player dunking a ball into the net. Its nickname is the "desert lynx" because it lives in dry areas and its ear tufts are similar to those of the lynx.

TAMING THE WILD ▶

The jungle cat is a wild cat known to raid chicken coops. This does not make it a welcome guest in the villages near its habitat. But the jungle cat's kittens can be easily tamed—a reminder that with some cats, at least, the difference between wild and tame can be a fine line.

▲ AQUA CAT

The fishing cat gets its name, of course, from fishing. This cat sits by the water and waits. If a fish comes by, it raises a paw and flips the unsuspecting prey onto the land and eats it. The fishing cat has webbed feet like a duck so it can swim better and hunt where most other cats will not bother —in the water.

SOFT SPOKEN

The clouded leopard is in a class by itself. It is not categorized as a big cat or small cat, but stands alone with the scientific name *neofelis nebulosa,* meaning new cat with a cloudy pelt. It has characteristics of both big and small cats. With especially long canine teeth, this cat has a fierce look but cannot roar. The clouded leopard is a purring cat.

CATS IN DANGER

VANISHED!

Species do vanish. They become extinct, never to be seen again. There are many reasons for this, but one underlying cause is that humans compete with animals for living space. As more people fill the globe, pressure is put on the wildlife that remains. Cats, so powerful in their own domain, lead fragile and endangered lives. Today, they need the help of humans to survive.

PRESERVED WITH CARE

At the beginning of this century, India alone had over 40,000 tigers. By the 1970's there were barely 7,000 wild tigers left. But people began to realize that these magnificent creatures are valuable to mankind. So India and other countries created "preserves," large territories set aside just for animals. Tigers hunt there. Prey is abundant. And people watch their progress with concern and awe.

POISON PREY

Pollution is not just a problem for people. Animals suffer, too. Chemicals that are sprayed on crops to help farmers raise more food, or pollution from factories carried in the air, can seep into the ground and water of the environment. Cats, like the ocelot, who eat small animals can be harmed by the poisons in their prey.

◀ Because of their beautiful fur, ocelots have long been hunted by man.

DANGEROUS BEAUTY

For a cat, great beauty can bring grave danger. Majestic and beautiful cats like the jaguar and ocelot have always been hunted for their fur. It is now illegal in most countries to kill wild cats. But "poachers," illegal hunters, still do.

guars

▲ The Asiatic lion once roamed a wide area of the Middle East and India. Today, only a few still exist, living on one small game pre-serve in India.

Cheetahs

HABITAT HUNGRY

Animals are dying because cities, villages, and farms are taking up more of their habitats, the natural surroundings they depend on for food and shelter. Meat-eaters, like the mother cheetah who has to feed hungry cubs, must wander for miles looking for prey. As her territory decreases, the chances of survival for her *and* her cubs grow slimmer.

Living high in the mountains of ▶ Central Asia, the snow leopard is still hunted for its thick fur coat.

THREATENED

Once, cougars were common in the western United States. But because they threatened cattle and sheep, many were killed. Now only a few thousand remain, and they are off-icially listed as a "threat-ened," though not yet endangered, species.

A cougar sub-species, the Florida panther, inhab-its the Florida Everglades and is very endangered. Less than 100 remain.

31

Photo Credits: Wolves & Coyotes

R.E. Barber: pages 35, 41, 43, 47, 52, 53
Erwin & Peggy Bauer: pages 48, 49, 53
Kit Breen: page 36
Tom Browning: page 52
Alan & Sandy Carey: pages 38, 44, 49, 50, 51
Henry Holdsworth: pages 52
Tom & Pat Leeson: pages 34, 35, 36, 38, 39, 41, 43, 47, 48, 50
John & Ann Mahan: pages 36, 37, 42, 44, 49
Rick McIntyre: pages 39, 42, 47,
Lynn Rogers: pages 36, 42, 46
Victoria Hurst/First Light: page 53
Thomas Kitchin/First Light: pages 34, 43, 46
Peter McLeod/First Light: page 35, 36, 38, 40, 44, 45, 46
Jim Zuckerman/First Light: page 37
Robert Lankinen/Wildlife Collection: pages 45
A. Maywald/Wildlife Collection: page 48
Michael Evan Sewell/Visual Pursuit: page 50
Michael Francis/Wildlife Collection: pages 35, 51, 53

Wolves and Coyotes

WOLF!

Dangerous. If we know very little about wolves, this word seems to fit. But wolves are not dangerous to people. They are wild and fierce, like any other animal that hunts to feed itself. And, like all animals, they have their own way of life—separate from humans.

DOG YEARS

The wolf, as it is now, roamed the earth over one million years ago. It *evolved*, or formed, from *carnivores* (meateaters) more than 100 million years ago. It is the original dog. In fact, it was about twenty million years ago that the dog, or *Canidae* family, developed from the wolf.

COLORFUL COAT ▶

Although known as the gray wolf, its coat is anything but plain gray. The variety of coat colors ranges from pure black to white, with shades of red, yellow, tan, silver, and brown in between. Any of these colors can occur within the very same family.

LUPUS AND RUFUS

Scientists have thought for some time that there are two types of wolves—the gray wolf, whose scientific name is *Canis lupus*, and the red wolf, known as *Canis rufus*. The gray wolf has lived over much of the northern hemisphere, but the red wolf has lived only in the southeastern United States.

Red wolf ▲

◀ Gray wolves that live in the high arctic are called arctic wolves.

BIG?

"Big" is not exactly the right word for wolves. They vary in size. The average male weighs 95 pounds and the female, 10 pounds less. They stand $2^{1}/_{2}$ feet high and measure 5 to $6^{1}/_{2}$ feet from the tip of the nose to the end of the tail.

HELPFUL HUNTERS

Wolves live in the mountains, forests, and plains of the northern hemisphere. They have a special role in relation to their environment. It's called their *ecological niche* (pronounced NICH). Wolves are the most numerous of all predators that hunt large mammals in this territory.

REAL CHARACTERS

Like dogs, wolves are very intelligent animals and are capable of learning. Also, each one seems to have its own personality. Some are shy, while others are bold and outgoing. Some are very social within their group, while others hang back.

MEMBERS OF THE PACK

Wolves have a strong social nature. They live as a family, in what is called a *pack*. There is a pecking order within the pack, in which each wolf has a rank. Some wolves are *dominant*— aggressive and forceful. Others are *submissive*, giving in to authority.

A wolf family—called a pack

BLOOD TIES

A male and female head the wolf pack. They are the core of a group that is related by blood and affection. Other members are their offspring, ranging in age from pups to two or three years old. Most packs have six or seven members, although some may include as many as 15 wolves.

NUMERO UNO

The most powerful male wolf in a pack is known as the alpha (Alpha is the first letter in the Greek alphabet). His mate, the alpha female, helps rule the pack. They have forceful personalities, necessary for their dominant role. They make the decisions that affect the pack's survival.

FANG FIGHTS

Wolves within a pack rarely fight, because the alphas maintain order. However, wolves do fight members of other packs or intruding lone wolves. All wolf packs have a territory of their own. They patrol it and mark it, so that other wolves will know to stay out. If a strange wolf intrudes, it will be attacked and killed.

THE LONE WOLF

Do you know a "lone wolf," someone who stays apart? The expression comes from wolves who go off on their own. A pack grows and changes. Some young adults wait to move up to alpha positions when leaders become old or weak. Other wolves leave to wander and hunt alone, but they may start their own pack if they can find a lone mate.

OMEGA

In larger packs, there are wolves known as omegas (Omega is the last letter in the Greek alphabet). These wolves are picked on by all members of the pack. Sometimes they are bothered so much that they leave the pack.

An angry alpha tells an unwelcome intruder, "Get off my turf!"

PACK CONTROL

If two wolves are going to rule a pack, they have to be able to show their authority and keep the others in line. To do so, they constantly dominate the lower-ranking wolves, from the moment these wolves are born. The alpha male dominates the other males, and the alpha female keeps the other females in line.

▲(1)The alpha wolf growls at a lower-ranking wolf, who lowers his head.

KIN PIN

Lower-ranking wolves (subordinates) are constantly disciplined by alphas. Alphas growl, bite, chase, and even pin them to the ground while the rest of the pack looks on (1-4).

(2)The alpha bites and tackles ▲ the subordinate.

(3)The alpha pins the ▶ subordinate.

TOP TAIL

A wolf's tail is like a flag waving its rank. Alphas hold theirs high. Wolves below the alphas keep their tails low. And lowest-ranking members tuck their tails between their legs.

▲ This male alpha wolf is holding his tail high.

▲ With her tail tucked between her legs, this subordinate female slinks off.

STERN STARE

A stern, unwavering stare from an alpha wolf is enough to convince members of the pack to bend to his or her authority. Submissive wolves will pull their lips back in a defensive grin, lower themselves to the ground, and, if they can, turn and slink away. Sometimes they roll on their backs to make things very clear that they know who's boss.

YOU'RE THE BOSS

Lower-ranking members show respect and affection for the alpha wolf in a special greeting ceremony. They approach him or her with their bodies low, fur and ears flattened. Then, reaching up, they lick and nip the alpha's face affectionately.

(4)Finally, the lower-ranking wolf begs forgiveness. ▼

39

WOLF TALK

Wolves are among the most loyal of animals, having deep attachments to their companions. Through gestures and body movements, wolves communicate their feelings. This "wolf talk" keeps the pack together and working as a group.

Affection between wolves is shown by nuzzling, licking, and cuddling.

BEGGING FOR BITES

The alpha wolves are usually at the head of the pack when attacking prey. They are the first ones to take bites out of the kill and get the choicest parts to eat. Lower-ranking wolves have to beg for food. They lay their ears back and, with their mouth closed, whine and paw at the alpha's face. Every now and then, they manage to grab some food.

40

PALS THAT HOWL

To people, the howl of the wolf is the sour of the wild. To wolves, it may be a party. Wolves most often howl as a pack—to encou age their closeness, to celebrate a successful hunt, to find separated members, and to tell other packs to keep back. On a calm night, howling can broadcast 120 square miles.

Alpha wolves make it clear to others that they should wait their turn to eat.

TELLTALE TAIL

A wolf also uses its tail to express how it's feeling. A tail raised and slightly curving up at the tip means the wolf is sure of itself. If the tail is dropped but curved up at the end, the wolf is being friendly. If the tail is between the wolf's legs, the wolf is being friendly or is afraid.

FACE TO FACE

Wolves have very expressive faces. A fearful wolf flattens its ears and covers its teeth in a meek smile. An angry wolf bares its teeth and points its ears forward. A wolf that is threatened and afraid keeps its ears back but also bares its teeth, letting its tongue roll out. These are clear messages, and pack mates know how to react to keep the peace.

This wolf is being threatened and is afraid.

One wolf sits down to show the other that he doesn't want to fight.

41

BUILT FOR HUNTING

At this very moment, wolves are hunting. They are physically built to do so. If there is snow, they are leaving a neat line of single tracks, hind feet following exactly behind front feet. This gait occurs because a wolf's legs are spaced very close together. It is an advantage in deep snow and difficult country.

TEETH FOR TOOLS

Teeth are weapons, and wolves have an arsenal of forty-two. Four pointed canines curve out near the front of the jaw, two on top and two on bottom. With these two-inch spikes, a wolf can pierce through tough hides and thick hair and hang on. With their *carnassials*, or molars, adult wolves can crush the thigh bone of a moose.

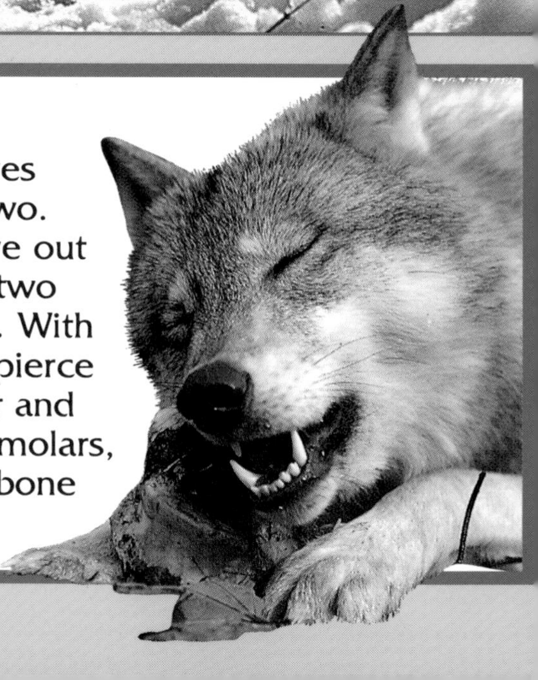

ON THEIR TOES

When wolves hunt, they are swift and silent—because they run on their toes. Like horses and cats, wolves keep the back parts of their feet raised when walking or running. Moving in such a way, with strong, muscular legs, wolves have long strides. They can trot for long periods at five miles an hour and race up to 40 miles an hour.

WOLF PARKA

In order to hunt in winter, wolves are protected by a fur coat as thick as three inches. Nearest to the wolf's flesh is a dense woolly undercoat to keep it warm. Black-tipped guard hairs form a longer, rougher outer-coat that shuts out moisture and sheds water. In this fur-lined raincoat, a wolf can go anywhere.

RADAR EARS

Hearing is a hunting skill, and wolves have the best. Wolves listen by turning their ears from side to side. By recogniz-ing where the sound is loudest, they can tell the direction the noise is coming from. Ears up, they can hear sounds several miles away.

THE NOSE KNOWS

Noses to the air, wolves pick up the scent of prey before they detect it in any other way. If the wind is blowing from the direction of the hunted animal, they can catch the odor as much as a mile and a half away—before they hear or see their prey. Noses down, wolves can also follow fresh tracks with their sharp sense of smell.

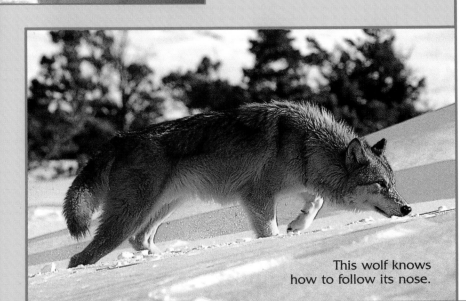

This wolf knows how to follow its nose.

43

PACK HUNTERS

Wolves are carnivores (meat-eaters). They are predators that hunt in groups. Sometimes a small animal like a beaver, rabbit, mouse, or bird is a mouthful for a single, hungry wolf. But in order to feed its many members, a pack must kill large prey, such as deer, caribou, elk, moose, or mountain sheep.

DELICATE BALANCE

Wolves are part of nature's scheme. Generally, they kill the old, sick, and young of their prey.

Often, the group on which they prey benefits as well. If the sick die, there is less chance of disease spreading. If older animals are killed, there is more food for the young. This "balance of nature" helps keep predator and prey healthy.

GETAWAY PREY

Fierce as wolves may seem, most of their prey escapes. Less than 10% of wolf hunting is successful. In one three-day study, wolves pursued 131 moose but killed only six. What happens? Deer and caribou can outrun wolves. Moose may fight back. That's 1200 pounds of animal with sharp antlers and heavy hooves—enough to crush a wolf's skull.

Usually, bison will defend themselves by grouping and greeting wolves head-on, with weight and horns. Wolves then try to separate one from the herd.

CLEAN PLATE

Food is life, but food is scarce for many wolves. Wolves can survive for two weeks without eating—and gorge themselves when they do. (An adult wolf can eat as much as 20 pounds at one time). Bolting down the flesh of its kill in large pieces, a pack of wolves leaves nothing behind—only the hooves and largest bones.

◀ A wolf is marking its territory.

WE ARE HERE. DON'T INTERFERE.

Survival depends on hunting grounds, and wolves will fight to defend them. A pack's territory ranges from 30 square miles to 800 square miles, depending on the kind of animal they hunt. Borders are posted with scent markings—urine sprayed on tree stumps and rocks—and advertised with group howling.

BURIED TREASURE ▲

Sometimes wolves will store some of their kill by dropping it in a hole and covering it over. Later, when hunting is difficult, they go back to this cache (sounds like "cash") and dig up their buried treasure.

PUPPY LOVE

For a wolf pack, new life begins in the spring, when pups are born. Usually, it is the alpha female that has the pups. She is pregnant for nine weeks and takes care of the pups for the first month. After that, the whole pack joins in the responsibility, helping feed them and watch out for them.

◀ A two-month-old wolf, now a member of the pack.

▼ A mother nurse her pups until the are old enough eat mea

LITTLE LITTER

Blind, deaf, and weighing only one pound—that's a wolf puppy at birth. But the litter of five or six pups grows quickly. At two weeks their eyes open. At three weeks, they weigh as much as seven pounds each and walk on all four legs. At about one month, the pups step out into the world.

DUG OUT

Wolf puppies are born underground in a den. Not just a hole in the ground, a den is a well-planned burrow that is dug by the mother. There's an entrance, just big enough for an adult wolf, and a tunnel at least ten feet long. At the end is a chamber where the pups are born.

▲ A mother watches out for her two nine-week-old pups outside the den.

With a wolf pup and its mother, affection begins early on.

STOMACH STORAGE

To keep her newborn pups warm, the mother wolf has to remain in the den for three weeks after giving birth. Once the pups can eat meat, she and other pack members bring it back to them—carrying it up to 20 miles in their stomachs. The adults then have to "bring up" the food so the pups can eat it!

♥ ♥ ♥ ♥ ♥ ♥ ♥ ♥ ♥ ♥ ♥

PUP-SITTERS

Once the pups leave the den, the whole pack becomes their protectors. The adult and juvenile wolves watch for predators—like eagles—and keep the pups from wandering off. This caretaking helps bond the newest members to the rest of the pack.

These wolf pups are playing tug-of-war, which will strengthen their bite.

BUSY BODIES

Running, chasing, pouncing, fighting, chewing—all this playing is serious fun for pups. It's how pups strengthen their muscles and develop hunting skills. In playing, they show their personalities, too. One "top dog" pup will want to boss his brothers and sisters around.

47

WOLVES AND PEOPLE

Who's afraid of the big, bad wolf? Most of us. Think of the wolves in the stories *Little Red Riding Hood* and *The Three Little Pigs.* For centuries, folktales have presented wolves as evil. In truth, wolves don't harm people. People kill wolves. And wolves are a threat only to people's livestock—their sheep, cattle, and chickens.

A SAD HISTORY

In the United States, a campaign to kill wolves was launched after Europeans began settling the land. In the 1800's, people moving into the Great Plains hunted buffalo, which the wolves had always depended on for food. The wolves, therefore, turned to cattle and sheep. To protect their livestock, ranchers started killing the wolves. Perhaps one to two million were killed. Today, there are probably fewer than 10,000 wolves in the United States, and most of them are in Alaska. Canada has as many as 50,000.

Mexican wolves, now endangered, once roamed Arizona, New Mexico, and Mexico.

WOLF RALLY

At one time, wolves lived throughout North America, Europe, and Asia. Outside of Alaska and Minnesota, they have been nearly eliminated from the United States. However, in 1973, the U.S. government passed the Endangered Species Act to protect those animals disappearing from the Earth. In addition, the government has appointed special wolf recovery teams for the Mexican, northern Rocky Mountain, eastern timber, and red wolves.

48

RANCHERS ROAR

The goal of wildlife biologists is to return wolves to their natural habitats—to places such as Yellowstone National Park. But ranchers and farmers who live near these areas protest because they fear for their livestock.

These wolves have brought down a moose.

WOLF vs. HUNTER

People who hunt big game, like elk and moose, usually go to a specific area, where they use lodges, restaurants, and guides. The people living in this area depend on the business provided by hunters. And they believe that wolves interfere with their livelihood by killing elk, moose, and other big game.

RESCUING RED

Once common in the southeastern United States, the red wolf is nearly extinct—gone forever. Many of the ones that have survived have mated with coyotes. In 1975, in an effort to save red wolves, 400 were captured to be bred and reintroduced into the Southeast. Only 14 of those caught were pure red wolves.

European wolf

Red wolf

ON THE RADIO

These days, wolves need people to care about them. Conservationists work to save animals and their environment. Wildlife biologists study animals. Wolf collars with radio transmitters help keep track of wolves so that scientists can help the wolves and learn more about them.

A scientist visits a pack living in a wolf park.

COYOTE COUNTRY

Although they live only in North America, coyotes are found from Alaska to Costa Rica, throughout Canada, and from the Pacific coast to the Atlantic. They live in Death Valley, California, where the temperature soars to 135°F, and on the plains of Canada, where it drops to -65°F. Today, there are more coyotes than ever before.

IN GOOD VOICE

Coyotes are musical. Their voices have a high and low range. Their howling is very close to singing, with a variety of sounds— barks, huffs, yelps, woofs, and yaps. They recognize each other's voices. When one coyote begins howling, others within hearing distance join in. Mated coyotes keep in touch through howling when separated. They even have a greeting song.

UP TO SIZE

The average coyote is two fe high, four feet long (including i tail), and looks like a medium-sized dog, similar to a German shepherd. Twenty-five pounds the average weight, although some are as heavy as 70 pounds. Whatever the size, thic fur makes coyotes look larger than they are.

COYOTE COUPLES

Coyotes are social animals that live in family groups. A male and female mate for life or, at least, may stay together for several years. They become much closer in the month before breeding. They hunt together, sing howling duets, and show affection by pawing and nuzzling.

Playing is a way of showing affection.

THE LONE COYOTE

Born in the spring, most coyote pups leave their parents by the fall. They go off to find their own hunting territories. If their parents' area has limited food sources and a large coyote population, they may have to go as far as 100 miles away. They may find mates, raise families, and live six to eight years.

Coyotes are less than one year old when they leave their parents.

These pups are taking a peek at the world from the door of their den.

NIGHT MOVES

Coyotes are excellent parents, guarding their pups carefully. If they suspect that their den is threatened, coyotes will move the pups to another place. Normally, this is nearby. But one female was observed carrying her four pups, one at a time, to a new den five miles away. That's a 40-mile journey in one night.

51

Trotting is a coyote's favorite way to travel.

A coyote blends in with the scenery—until it jumps out and flashes its teeth. ▼

ON THE MOVE

Coyotes are natural wanderers, often traveling up to 50 miles in a single night. If they trot, they can average 20 miles per hour (mph). When they gallop, they can reach 30 mph. Sometimes they run 40 mph—in short spurts. That's fast enough to catch a jackrabbit.

◀ Coyotes can
up to 14 feet

CAMOUFLAGE COAT

Coyotes have coats that keep them undercover, so they can sneak up on prey and hide from predators. The ones that live in wooded regions have dark fur, which makes them difficult to see in the underbrush. Desert-dwelling coyotes have tawny coats that blend in with sand and weathered rock.

BUILT JUST RIGHT

Coyotes have the tools to be excellent hunters. With their powerful legs, they can leap up to 14 feet. With keen eyesight, they can see the slightest movement yards away. With their sharp hearing, they can detect the faintest stirrings of mice under the snow. And with a strong sense of smell, they can pick up a human scent and run away to safety.

FULL MENU

Coyotes are not fussy about their food. Scavengers, they will steal a meal stored by other predators. They eat deer, rabbits and other rodents, insects, and fish. They will even plunge into the water after frogs, crayfish, and turtles. Although they are meat-eaters, they will also eat fruits and berries, and they have a special fondness for watermelon.

▲ This coyote is making a meal out of some berries.

◄ A coyote raiding a chicken coop.

A coyote caught in a trap.

Coyotes have the ears and nose for detecting even the smallest creatures. ▼

SUCCESSFUL SURVIVORS

According to one Native American legend, coyotes will be the last living animal on Earth. In some ways, this is hard to imagine. Ever since the West was settled by non-Indians, people and coyotes have been in conflict. Coyotes eat livestock, such as cattle, sheep, and chickens. Shot, trapped, and poisoned by angry farmers, millions of coyotes have died. Somehow, though, they have "learned" to avoid human hunters.

THE WILY COYOTE

Coyotes are clever hunters who some-times hunt in pairs. One of their favorite prey is the jackrabbit, which tends to run in circles. One coyote will chase the rabbit while the other waits at the head of the circle. It's not likely that the rabbit will live to make too many circles.

Photo Credits: Bears

Breck P. Kent: pages 57, 60, 67, 78-79
Susan Lang: pages 76-77
Tom & Pat Leeson: pages 56-59, 62, 64, 65, 68-69, 72, 73, 74-77, 79
Zig Leszczynski: pages 59, 63, 68, 75
Lynn M. Stone: page 74
Fred Bruemmer/DRK: page 61
Johnny Johnson/DRK: pages 56, 60, 62, 63, 66, 70-71
Stephen J. Krasemann/DRK: pages 61, 65
Dwight R. Kuhn/DRK: page 78
Wayne Lynch/DRK: pages 56, 59, 60, 63, 68, 71, 72, 78-79
John W. Matthews/DRK: page 78
Leonard Lee Rue III/DRK: page 66
Belinda Wright/DRK: page 58
Mark Newman/International Stock: page 69, 70, 71
Will Regan/International Stock: page 65
Ron Sanford/International Stock: page 66
Tom Edwards/Visuals Unlimited: page 57
Ken Lucas/Visuals Unlimited: page 60
Joe McDonald/Visuals Unlimited: pages 67, 69, 75
Erwin C. "Bud" Nielsen/Visuals Unlimited: page 67
William J. Weber/Visuals Unlimited: page 58
Michael Francis/Wildlife Collection: pages 56, 73
John Guistina/Wildlife Collection: pages 59, 69
Martin Harvey/Wildlife Collection: page 58
Henry Holdsworth/Wildlife Collection: page 75
Robert Lankinen/Wildlife Collection: pages 70, 71
Dean Lee/Wildlife Collection: page 77
Gary Schultz/Wildlife Collection: pages 57, 73
Jack Swenson/Wildlife Collection: page 64
Tom Vezo/Wildlife Collection: page 64
Wide World Photos: page 79

Scientific Consultant:
Gary Brown
National Park Ranger
And Bear-Management Specialist

BEARS

WILD BEARS

These amazing creatures are some of the largest land animals on earth. One of nature's wildest wonders, bears swim, climb, run at surprisingly high speeds, and travel great distances in one day.

This fun-loving grizzly enjoys a roll in a field of berries. ▶

NOT TOO CLOSE

People like to think of bears as cute and cuddly. But bears like to stay far away from people. If startled or provoked, a bear may even attack.

WALKING UPRIGHT ▼

A bear usually walks on all fours. But a curious bear will stand up on its back legs to get a better view or to pull down food from above. To defend itself, a bear will rear up and lash out with its massive paws.

◀ BIG DIET

Bears are big eaters. They are classified as *carnivores,* or meat-eaters, but all have a diet that includes plants. They may also dine on honey, mushrooms, and many other things.

56

► Through bear talk, cubs learn from their mother.

▼ Brown bears roar when they're really angry.

NOT A BEAR
The Australian koala bear is not a member of the bear family at all. A marsupial like the kangaroo, the koala carries and nurses its young in a stomach pouch.

CHATTER ▲
Although they are fairly quiet, bears do communicate with sound. They growl when threatened and hum when content. They even whine and cry when they're upset.

LIVING ALONE
Bears rule wherever they live. Their only enemies, besides people, are other bears. Solitary creatures, they usually avoid one another. Only when it's time to mate do adult males and females get together. A mother bear, however, may spend a couple of years with her cubs.

57

BEAR COUNTRY

Ever wonder if there are bears living nearby? They might be! Bears can be found on all continents except Africa, Antarctica, and Australia. There are eight living species, which come in a variety of colors.

BROWN BEAR

Found in Europe, in Asia as far south as India, in western Canada, Alaska, and parts of the western United States, brown bears have the greatest range of all. They are also some of the largest bears, weighing over 800 pounds on average and measuring up to 10 feet from nose to tail.

ASIATIC BLACK BEAR

The Asiatic black bear lives in brushlands and forests throughout Asia, including Japan and the island of Taiwan.

BLACK BEAR

The tree-climbing black bear inhabits forests, swamps, and wooded mountains from Alaska and Canada down to Mexico and Florida.

POLAR BEAR

As wintry white as the ice and snow of the North Pole, the polar bear inhabits Arctic areas in Norway, Greenland, Russia, Canada, and Alaska.

SLOTH BEAR
The sloth bear lives throughout the Indian subcontinent, from Nepal and Bhutan down to Sri Lanka. A fairly small bear, it has a white or yellow "necklace" on its black chest.

SPECTACLED BEAR
There's only one bear that lives in South America, and that's the spectacled bear. This unique creature, which gets its name from the markings around its eyes, roams along the Andes Mountains in Venezuela, Colombia, Ecuador, Peru, and Bolivia.

SUN BEAR
Smallest of all the bears, the sun bear averages 100 pounds and measures about four feet long. It keeps to the dense Southeast Asian forests of Sumatra, Borneo, the Malayan Peninsula, Myanmar, and Thailand.

GIANT PANDA
The giant panda makes its home in the high mountains of central China, where bamboo, its favorite food, is plentiful. The rare panda is confined to an area only 300 miles long and about 80 miles wide.

BIG BODIES

How would you describe a bear? Look carefully. Most bears have a large head with a long snout, small close-set eyes, and erect ears. Their heavily built body has short, thick limbs and a stumpy tail. And, yes, they are big and furry!

Talk about big! There once was a polar bear that weighed over 2,000 pounds and measured 11 feet long.

FANTASTIC FUR
Fairly uniform in color, bear fur can be either black, white, or many shades of brown. But several species have light-colored markings on their chest that accent their size when they rear up to fight or defend themselves.

▲ GRIN AND BEAR IT
Most bears have 42 teeth. Their sharp canines can tear flesh from a carcass, while their broad, flat molars allow them to grind down plants.

Unlike the claws of most cats, a bear's claws can't be pulled in when not in use.

NEARSIGHTED ▶
Bears are built for seeing small things close at hand, such as berries and other food. In fact, they are fairly nearsighted and sometimes get so absorbed in eating that they don't see an approaching person. Hikers often whistle or wear bells to alert bears of their presence.

KILLER CLAWS ▲
A bear's foot comes equipped with five long, curved claws. Bears use these sharp, all-purpose claws to mark or climb trees, dig for food, excavate their dens, rip apart prey, scratch, or defend themselves.

◀ BODY LANGUAGE

Bears not only use their body for movement, but also to communicate. A stare from a bear is a serious threat. But when a bear lowers its head, that means it wants peace. Bears also mark trees or other objects in their territory with their scent or claw marks.

NOSING AROUND

Smell is probably a bear's greatest sense. Like a bloodhound, it can accurately sniff out a trail where prey walked many hours before. It can also pick up a scent from the air and find the source miles and miles away.

FAST FEET

They may look slow and clumsy, but bears walk like people—on the soles of their feet, with heels touching the ground. Some are also fast runners. Brown bears can reach speeds of up to 40 miles per hour—faster than any Olympian sprinter and as fast as a greyhound!

STAYING COOL ▶

During the summer, bears have to stay cool, especially polar bears, which are built for very cold weather. They spread out and expose their massive body to the air or ice.

▶This sleepy polar bear cools itself off in some arctic slush.

LEAVING THE DEN

When spring arrives, bears leave their den to search for food. During their first weeks outside, when the only available food may be grasses, herbs, and twigs, bears tend to lose weight. Adults also shed their thick coats so they'll be cooler in the summer months ahead.

In Alaska, ▶ this bear is enjoying a meal of blueberries.

HARVEST TIME

In the forest, as new foods ripen in late summer, the bear family gorges on berries, fruits, and nuts. They spend more and more time eating, storing up a thick layer of fat to provide energy and extra insulation during the long winter months.

The fruit of a rose, called ▶ a rose hip, is a tasty treat for a grizzly bear cub.

FINDING A MATE

For several months in the spring, bears leave their solitary habits behind to seek out a mate. Courtship may include vicious fights among competing males. Mating bears sometimes spend a few days together, but the males soon leave to seek out another female.

These two male grizzly bears are preparing to fight.

TO THE DEN
In the fall, bears begin their task of homemaking. Female polar bears dig their winter home in snowbanks. The Asiatic black bear makes a bed of fresh twigs on the forest floor. Grizzlies dig out homes underground, chewing off branches to build springy mattresses. Black bears find a denning space underneath rotting logs.

◀ A black bear mother and cub cuddle up in their den.

A black bear mother ▶
nursing her two little cubs.

WINTER BABIES
Cubs are born during the winter in the shelter of a den. Very tiny at birth, the cubs spend the first weeks of their lives nursing and sleeping.

Polar bear cubs snuggle ▶
into the warmth of
their mother's fur.

READY FOR SLEEP
When a bear enters its winter den, it is fat, has a thick coat, and is ready for sleep. Body temperature lowers and heart rate decreases. Cubs that spend more than one season with their mother accompany her into the den, but otherwise a bear sleeps alone.

63

EATING EVERYTHING

Bears are omnivorous—they will gobble down just about anything in sight. And that may be the secret to their success—they are not fussy eaters and can find a tasty meal just about anywhere.

▼ Not great hunters, black bears eat mostly plant matter, including grass, berries, acorns, roots, and herbs.

A SEASONAL DIET

A bear's diet may change from season to season—the tender roots or shoots of spring plants, ripe summer berries and fruit, and acorns in the fall. In the spring, bears also eat trees, peeling away the bark to get at the inner layer, called *cambium*.

EATING MEAT

Bears are not the great killers many people think they are. They do catch and eat small animals, and some, like the polar bear, eat more meat than others. But when it comes to eating larger prey, bears mostly feed on animals that are already dead.

◀ On the coast of Alaska, this hungry grizzly attacks a razor clam.

FISHING

Alaskan brown bears are great at fishing. They grab fish in their mouth or pin them down with their front paws. They even leap from overhanging boulders and plunge into the water to nab a passing fish. Gathering at streams and rivers during the salmon run, brown bears may eat as much as 90 pounds of fish in one day!

▼ PATIENT HUNTER

The predatory polar bear has several hunting techniques. In one, called "still hunting," the bear sniffs out a seal's "breathing hole" and then may wait patiently for hours above it. When a seal surfaces for air, the bear instantly delivers a powerful blow, grabs with its sharp, pointed teeth, and hauls it out of the water.

▼ UNHAPPY CAMPERS

When a bear is around, nothing edible is safe. Campers come out of their tents in the morning to find packages of food ripped open, jars smashed, and coolers overturned. The best remedy is to buy "bear-proof" containers or hang the food out of reach.

IN THE DUMPS

Garbage dumps are an open invitation to hungry bears. As the bears lose their fear of people and become more dependent upon them for food, they may actually become more dangerous.

CUTE CUBS

A mother bear gives birth in her winter den to one or two babies that weigh only a few ounces. Covered with a thin, fuzzy layer of hair, they are blind and completely helpless. After surviving the winter on rich, fatty milk, bear cubs will leave the den in spring and go out into the world with their mother.

◀ Only 10 days old and weighing 30 ounces, these grizzly cubs will grow to about 150 pounds in their first year.

MOM KNOWS BEST ▶

When it comes to learning the secrets of bear life, a cub's only teacher is its mother. By following, watching closely, and imitating her actions, cubs learn everything they need to know—how to hunt, where to find berries or a fishing stream, how to dig for ants or get honey from a beehive.

KEEPING A DISTANCE ▲

A cub's worst enemy is another bear. If a cub comes too close to an adult male, it risks being attacked and killed. Mother bears have to be fiercely protective of their babies and do everything they can to keep them away from older males.

PLAYTIME

Playing is an important part of a young bear's life. When playfighting, cubs will stand up and try to push one another off balance. But if play becomes too rough, a cub can stop everything by flattening its ears and giving out a low warning sound.

Although climbing is a fun kind of play, it's also a way to get at food and escape danger.

◄ LEAVING HOME

Some cubs remain with their mother for up to three years, denning with her in the winter. Others are on their own after a year. Once they leave, cubs may stay together for a few months or go their separate ways. They've learned the basics, and now it's time to live a bear's life.

67

FOUR LITTLE BEARS

Take a look at the spectacled, sun, sloth, and Asiatic bears. They're the smallest of all bears, and they are very unique.

A mother sun bear and her cub.

SUN BEAR

The sun bear is the smallest of the bears—about 3 to 4 and a half feet long and 100 pounds.

Some people try to make this little black bear a pet, only to discover later that it's uncontrollable. The sun bear is one of the most dangerous animals in its territory.

TROUBLEMAKER ▲

Of all the bears, the Asiatic black is most likely to make trouble with people living in its territory. It has been known to raid herds of cattle, sheep, and goats, and to destroy crops. It also has a reputation for being ill-tempered and has attacked people.

▼ A sun bear snoozing in a tree.

FRUIT LOVER ▶

If there's one thing the South American spectacled bear loves, it's fruit. After building a platform from branches high in a fruit-laden tree, it will settle in for days of feasting. When it has eaten all the fruit within reach, it picks up and moves to a new site.

▼ The spectacled bear.

LIVING VACUUM ▼

The sloth bear loves termites, its staple food. To get at them, it digs a hole in the nest, sticks its muzzle in, and blows violently to clean the surrounding area. Closing its nostrils, it then sucks in the insects. The sounds a sloth bear makes while vacuuming up its meal can be heard 200 yards away!

When playfighting, ▶ sloth bears can look pretty fierce. But unlike most bears, they actually like the company.

◀ TOP OF THE CLASS

Captive sun bears have proven their intelligence in amazing ways. One young bear figured out how to use its huge, curved claw as a key, unlocking a cupboard and taking out a sugarbowl. Another scattered rice from its dish to attract chickens, which it then killed and ate.

NORTHERN GIANTS

Amidst the ice floes of the Arctic Circle lives the polar bear—the king of the north. This bear reaches gigantic sizes, and does so by eating meat. A skilled hunter, the polar bear has been known to attack beluga whales, jumping on their back, then riding them under the sea.

MEAT EATERS

Polar bears live almost entirely on ringed seals. Other prey might include a walrus calf, a musk-ox, fish, or a whale. During the brief Arctic summer, they move onto land and eat whatever plants, small mammals, birds, and bird eggs they can find.

DOG-PADDLING

Almost invisible on the white ice, the polar bear can stalk a resting seal. Or, by using its webbed paws to "dog-paddle" towards its prey, it can dive underwater for as long as two minutes, then launch itself as far as eight feet into the air and land on the ice!

POLAR PALS

Instead of denning, male polar bears may stay active, hunting throughout the harsh winter. Sometimes they meet up with other polar bears and take time for a little fun. Playfighting is a way to develop their strength and hunting skills.

CURIOUS COAT

Perfectly insulated, the polar bear has a thick layer of fat under its skin and more fur than any other bear. Fur on the soles of its paws helps the bear grip ice. Surprisingly, polar bear fur is hollow. The hair collects light from the sun and channels the heat to the polar bear's black skin. Because the skin is black, it absorbs the heat.

A nap is a good way for polar bears to conserve energy in the cold Arctic.

SNOWY DENS

In the fall, females start digging their winter dens in the snowbanks. Warm air gets trapped inside, and drifting snow covers the opening. In late December or early January the female gives birth, usually to twins.

This polar bear cub stays warm inside its den.

MOM KNOWS BEST

When the polar bear family breaks out of the den in March or April, the cubs weigh about 22 pounds and have thick fur coats. For nearly two years they watch their mother closely, learning the hunting skills needed for survival.

ALL-AMERICAN

With its powerful body, the North American black bear can outrun a person, shinny up a tree with amazing speed, and easily break through dense underbrush in a forest. Although called a black bear, it comes in many colors, such as blue-black, brown, cinnamon, or even white.

SIZING UP

An adult male black bear is about 4 to 6 feet long when fully grown and can weigh up to about 580 pounds. As with most bear species, males are considerably larger than females.

CURLING UP ▼

Black bears usually curl up for the winter in a cave. Some of them will dig a den under the roots of a large tree. If the trees have been logged out, they make beds on the ground amongst thick vegetation, raking up leaves and plants to lie on.

GHOST BEAR

Found only in a small area of British Columbia, Canada, the Kermode bear is the white version of a black bear. Also called "ghost bears," Kermode bears are so rare that few people have actually seen them.

◀ UP A TREE

When a black bear cub leaves the den, its claws are already well developed. The cub needs them, because every time the mother bear senses danger, she will chase her cubs into the nearest tree.

A black bear mother ▶ and her cub.

BARE SOLES

Bears that stay on the ground most of the time, like polar bears, have feet with hairy soles. But black bears, which spend much of their life in trees, have bare soles. Along with sharp, narrow, curved claws, bare soles make it easier for the black bear to climb.

MIXED MENU ▶

The black bear is a powerful swimmer and good fisher. On land, the bear flips over stones and decayed logs to find insects and grubs. It digs out burrows to reach small rodents. It also feeds on vegetation, such as berries, and loves honey.

A black bear taking a swim.

MIGHTY BEAR

Brown bears rank among polar bears as the largest of all bears. The heaviest yet recorded weighed more than 2,000 pounds. Perhaps the best-known brown bear is the mighty grizzly. "Grizzled" means partly gray, which perfectly describes the gray-tipped hairs of a grizzly's shaggy coat.

TOP BEAR ▲

Spectacular fights occur between big, male brown bears when they are courting and when they gather at rivers to fish for migrating salmon. If the challenged bear does not turn his head and back up, the two go at each other with vicious lunges, slapping and biting until one bear gives up.

THE BROWN FAMILY

One of the largest brown bears is the Kodiak, found only on Kodiak Island in southern Alaska. Other brown bears include the Siberian bear, the red bear of northern India and the Himalayas, the Manchurian bear, the horse bear of Tibet and western China, and the Hokkaido bear of Japan.

◄ HUMPBACK

Ranging in color from light cream to black, brown bears are some-times confused with black bears. However, brown bears are larger, have round faces, and have a hump on their back. The hump is a mass of muscles that gives them added power for digging and fighting.

EVERY BITE

Grizzlies eat everything, including fungi, leaves, berries, roots, sprouting plants, insects, fish, and small mammals. When they find the carcasses of larger animals, like moose, elk, or livestock, they store the remains, returning again and again to the storage site until every last morsel is consumed.

AMAZING CLAWS

Grizzlies and other brown bears have enormous claws, which sometimes reach six inches in length. With these tools they do battle, dig, climb, handle food, and scratch. One very skilled grizzly was even seen handling a feather, turning it over and over in its paws.

▲ CUBSITTING

Grizzlies are not as solitary as was once thought. Female grizzlies will adopt motherless cubs and may even develop friendships. In the McNeil River area of Alaska, two females met one another almost every day and swapped cubs over an entire summer.

PANDA PALS

With its striking black-and-white image, the giant panda cannot be mistaken for any other bear. This national treasure of China is one of the most popular animals visited at zoos.

BAMBOO, PLEASE ▼

A giant panda may spend much of its time sitting and tearing off the coarse leaves and stems of bamboo, its favorite food. It may also eat a little grass, some flowering plants, or raid a beehive for honey. A special "thumb" on its front paws helps the giant panda grasp bamboo stems. Unique among bears, this false thumb is made up of an elongated wrist bone.

SEVERE MEASURES

Because of hunting and loss of habitat, the giant panda is endangered. Symbol of the World Wildlife Fund, the giant panda has a population fewer than 1,000. It is in such danger of extinction, the Chinese government has decreed that anyone killing a giant panda may be sentenced to death.

The red ▶
panda

◄ BEAR OR RACCOON?

For many years scientists wondered if the giant panda is a bear or a relative of the raccoon. The giant panda has many similarities to the smaller red panda, which *is* a member of the raccoon family. However, today, scientists classify the giant panda as a bear.

LITTLE GIANT

Despite its name, the giant panda measures only 27 to 31 inches tall from the ground to its shoulders. It's about five to six feet from nose to rump. In most bear species, males are considerably larger than females, but all adult giant pandas are nearly the same size. It's almost impossible to tell them apart.

LOOKING FOR A MATE

During mating season, giant pandas find one another by scent and sound. To advertise their presence, they rub their scent glands against trees. The male vocalizes with an eerie call, and the female responds with a sheep-like bleat.

BLACK-AND-WHITE BABIES

At birth, giant panda cubs weigh a mere 3 to 5 ounces. Within weeks they have developed a light version of the striking black-and-white panda coat. In a year they are on their own, and their mother gives birth again.

BEARS AND PEOPLE

Bears are not so much *a* danger as they are *in* danger. In the early 1800s, one explorer traveling in Colorado saw over 200 grizzly bears in one day. Today, there are probably fewer than 70,000 grizzlies in all of North America. As people log wilderness areas and plant crops, bears lose habitat. Also, bears are still hunted.

STUDY BUDDY

Scientists study a bear's needs in order to help provide for its survival. However, studying bears in the wild is usually difficult because they are such shy animals, and scarce. Researchers sometimes tag bears with radio collars in order to keep track of their movements.

Visiting bear country in a bus a good way to view wildli while avoiding attack

▲ POLAR PROTECTION

Hunting polar bears for sport was once so popular that in 1965 people had to band together to help save this magnificent creature from extinction. Today, only native peoples in Greenland and Alaska may hunt polar bears for their own use.

DANCING BEAR

For centuries, people have used bears for entertainment. Bears have performed in circuses, street acts, the movies and television. The ancient Romans used bears in their circuses, along with chariot races and warrior contests.

◀ People capture sloth bears and train them to perform.

SERIOUS ATTACK

Bear attacks on people are rare, but if people get too close, especially to a mother's cubs or to a bear's food, an attack is more likely. The bear will charge on all four legs, then strike with a bite or a claw.

A POPULAR IMAGE ▲

Cuddly bear characters are all around—in books, movies, and advertisements. One of the most popular images of all, Smokey the Bear, was created during World War II as an aid for fire prevention. Today, he is still at work reminding us with his slogan, "Remember, only you can prevent forest fires!"

THE TEDDY BEAR ▶

In 1902, President Teddy Roosevelt went hunting but had little success. So a captured black bear cub was brought out for him to shoot. The president refused, and the story touched the hearts of the people. Soon a small toy bear was created that became one of the most popular toys ever made—the "Teddy Bear."

▲ A black bear cub

79

Photo Credits: Apes & Monkeys

Francois Gohier: pages 87, 93, 95
Bob Jacobson: page 84
Tom & Pat Leeson: pages 97, 101
Zig Leszczynski: pages 82, 92, 98, 99
Mark Newman: pages 95, 100
Art Wolfe: pages 82, 84
Michael Durham/ENP: page 84
Gerry Ellis/ENP: pages 82, 85, 86, 87, 90, 91, 93, 94, 96, 99, 102, 104
Pete Oxford/ENP: pages 86
Terry Whittaker/ENP: pages 86, 92
Konrad Wothe/ENP: pages 100, 102, 105
Kenfre Inc./International Stock: page 91
Phillip Little/International Stock: page 101
UPI/Corbis-Bettman: page 105
A.J. Copley/Visuals Unlimited: page 82
Ken Lucas/Visuals Unlimited: pages 86, 90, 102, 103
Tom DiMauro/Wildlife Collection: pages 85, 92, 97
Martin Harvey/Wildlife Collection: pages 87, 92, 94, 96, 98, 104
Tim Laman/Wildlife Collection: pages 96, 104
Dean Lee/Wildlife Collection: page 103
Jack Swenson/Wildlife Collection: pages 82, 97, 105

Scientific Consultant:
Colleen M. McCann, PhD
Wildlife Conservation Society

Apes and Monkeys

Using its thumb an
fingers, this wool
monkey grasps
tree limb

◀ Great acrobats,
these two orangutans
hang tight for a kiss.

HUMANLIKE?

How closely related are apes and
monkeys to people? They, like us,
belong to a group of mammals
known as "primates." Primates
share certain traits. We have thumbs
that can grasp things, eyes posi-
tioned at the front of our head, and
a large brain. Also, apes and monkeys, like people, have a social life.

A WILD BUNCH

Apes and monkeys
do wild things like
beat their chest, swing
from trees, and howl
day and night. These
highly advanced crea-
tures also do much
more. They show feel-
ings of affection. They
fight and make up. Some
have even learned to use
tools.

8

▼ MONKEY SEE...

Talk about smart! Apes and monkeys are very fast learners. A young female macaque discovered that dunking a sweet potato in the sea was the easiest way to clean sand off. In a short time, her family and friends, then the entire group, started washing their potatoes.

THE SPECIAL ONE

The tarsier is in a group by itself. To *primatologists,* the people who study primates, this creature has a strange mix of traits. It has the large eyes and ears of the prosimians. But it also has a short, furry nose like monkeys and apes.

WHAT'S A LEMUR? ▲

The lemur is a prosimian—a relative of apes and monkeys. Found only on the island of Madagascar, the ring-tailed lemur looks more like a cat than a monkey—with its whiskers and large ears.

WHAT A LIFE!

Compared to many animals, monkeys and apes live a long time. In the wild, monkeys can live for 20 years or more, and gorillas, chimpanzees, and orangutans may live past the age of 40.

MANY MONKEYS

The world has so many monkeys, about 130 species. Those that live in South and Central America are called New World monkeys, and those found in Africa and Southeast Asia are called Old World monkeys.

A langur from Asia ▶

BIG AND BAD ▼
The largest monkeys, baboons, have a tough character, which comes in handy around the lions and hyenas in Africa. Baboons spend the day on the ground, but sleep in trees or cliffs at night for safety.

LITTLE CRITTER ▼
The smallest New World monkey is the pygmy marmoset, just 5 inches long with an 8-inch tail. It lives in the rain forests of several South American countries. Like other New World monkeys, it spends most of its time in trees.

COLORFUL DIANA
The Diana monkey is a member of the guenon family, the most common group of monkeys in Africa. Guenons have long arms, legs, and tails, and brightly colored coats.

84

ABSOLUTE APES

The ape family has just four members: gibbons, chimpanzees, orangutans and gorillas; the last three are known as the "great apes" due to their size and body shapes. They live only in Africa and parts of Southeast Asia.

▲ High above the forest floor, 20 to 100 feet, orangutans spend much of their day swinging from limb to limb looking for food.

APE OR ▲ MONKEY?

Besides their large size, apes are different from monkeys in other ways. They don't have a tail, and they "knuckle-walk" on their front hands. Monkeys scamper about on the flats of their palms, much like a squirrel.

ACROBAT

Smallest of the apes, the gibbon has very long arms for its size, and uses them to swing through the trees. It can also walk along a branch using only its two legs, holding both arms out for balance.

SUPER SILVERBACK

Apes are big—really big. The largest and most powerful of all is the gorilla. A mature male "silverback" stands more than 5^1/$_2$ feet tall and weighs an average of 350 pounds. Gorillas lead a quiet life, eating massive amounts of leaves, stems, bark, and roots.

LIVING ROOM

Apes and monkeys live in tropical forests and grasslands. They eat fruit, nuts, grass, leaves, insects, and other small animals.

The white-faced saki lives in South America's Amazon basin.

REAL SURVIVOR

In South Africa, the chacma baboon live in deserts and plains, as well as along the rocky seashore, where it feeds on crustaceans. At night it sleeps on boulders or rocky cliffs.

▼ STAY AWAY!

Each group of apes and monkeys needs a place to call its own. White-handed gibbon families live in the forests of Southeast Asia, and they don't like trespassers. Each morning the male and female sing a duet for as long as 15 minutes, sending a message to other gibbons to stay away!

OUT ON A LIMB ▼

In the dense canopy of Brazil's rain forest, the golden lion tamarin eats, sleeps, and travels. To avoid predators, most forest-dwelling monkeys, such as tamarins and marmosets, sleep in the hollows of trees— a tough spot for a jaguar to reach.

SNOW MONKEY

The Japanese macaque has adapted to a harsh environment. On rugged Honshu Island, these monkeys endure snowy winters in the mountains. Once the trees have shed their leaves, the macaque gets through the cold season by feeding on bark.

MOUNTAINEER

In the forests of Africa, lowland and mountain gorillas live peacefully, having no natural enemy except people. Lowland and mountain gorillas look somewhat different. Western lowland gorillas have short, black fur and broad faces. Gorillas from the Eastern lowlands are the largest, and have long faces and short, black fur. Mountain gorillas, like the one shown here, have long, silky black fur and big jaws.

AMAZING BODY

Apes and monkeys are built for a life of climbing, grasping branches, and collecting food.

TALENTED TAIL

Like many other monkeys, the spider monkey can grasp a tree limb with its tail and hang safely while collecting fru with both its hands.

SEEING STRAIGH

Like people, apes and mon keys have *stereoscopi* vision, which enables them to judge distances. That': very important if you're ar acrobat like the black-and white colobus monkey leaping from one branch tc another high above the ground

HANDY THUMB

Try to pick up a pencil using only your fingers, not your thumb. It's difficult. Using your opposable thumb makes it easier, because it can press against the fingers like a clamp. Apes and monkeys have a thumb, too, which helps them groom, pick leaves, and clamber up trees.

WISE GUY

Apes and monkeys are known for their intelligence. Next to people, gorillas and chimpanzees are thought to be the smartest of all animals. Chimps have even learned to strip twigs of leaves and use them to fish a termite dinner out of a nest.

ON THE MOVE

Monkeys can really move through the trees, but the ape known as the gibbon is the champion swinger. It makes spectacular leaps from one tree to another, or it *brachiates* (BRAY-kee-ates) from limb to limb—using its long, powerful arms. It grabs a branch and swoops downward, then reaches with the other hand for another limb, and keeps on swinging!

PADDED SEAT

Old World monkeys, such as baboons, sleep sitting up, and they have a built-in cushion for comfort. Look on each side of the tail and you can see their two hairless pads of skin, called *ischial callosites.*

The hair of apes and monkeys offers protection from rain, wind, and biting insects. It often needs cleaning, and fellow troop members are eager to groom a friend.

IN THE CHEEK

Some monkeys have a special place for storing food—in cheek pouches! Baboons, macaques, and other monkeys stuff food into the pouches and snack on it later!

89

TALK ABOUT IT

Great communicators, apes and monkeys have many ways of warning each other of danger. And they have many ways of letting family or group members know what's on their mind.

Howler monkeys are known for their howl, which sounds a little like a dog's bark and can be heard up to two miles away.

LIP ACTION

Lip-smacking is used by monkeys as a friendly invitation for another monkey to approach. Goeldi's monkey opens and closes its mouth rapidly, and sometimes even sticks its tongue out!

CHIMP PALS

Friendships among chimpanzees are very strong and can last for years and years, even if one chimp should take up with another group. When two chimp friends meet after a period of separation, they throw their arms around each other, hug and kiss, and pat each other on the back.

ENEMY ALERT

The vervet monkey of Africa has developed specific alarm calls for each of the major predators it faces: eagles, leopards, and snakes. Group members will look up at the sky, run up a tree, or quickly climb even higher into the trees, depending on which predator is at hand.

PASS IT ON

When apes and monkeys think of a solution to a problem, the word gets around. One group of chimps that learned to use twigs to fish for carpenter ants passed on this technology to another community living some distance away.

TOUGH GUY

Baboons are tough characters, and the leader of the troop is the toughest of all. Feared and respected by his fellow baboons, the leader may only need to glare at an upstart male or a youngster causing too much mischief—and the problem is solved.

FANGS

Watch out for those teeth! Apes and monkeys have pretty sharp canines, which are sometimes used to threaten other troop members, or to defend against outsiders.

GETTING TOGETHER

Most apes and monkeys live in groups, or troops, in which they grow up and develop close relationships. Group living offers protection. It also means following rules and resolving disagreements to keep the group together.

JUST US ▲

Gibbons like to keep their group small. The typical gibbon family has a mother, father, and as many as four offspring. The parents are very protective of their territory and will argue or even fight with other families over the boundaries.

MAKING UP

When a fight breaks out between members of a chimpanzee group, the dispute gets resolved. Chimps often make up within a half-hour. One chimp will approach the other with an outstretched arm or open hand.

Black-and-white colobus monkeys usually travel in small groups—one male with several females and their babies.

▼ REGROUPING
Spider monkeys form groups of about 20 members, but also break into smaller groups to forage for food.

CLEANING UP
For apes and monkeys, grooming is a great way to get rid of any dirt or insects caught in their hair. But most importantly, grooming establishes and strengthens relationships. Some monkeys spend as much as five hours each day grooming.

SOCIAL LADDER ▶
Macaque society is very well organized, with every member having a rank. High-ranking members eat first, take the best resting spot, and travel in the center of the group. Each monkey inherits its status from its mother but, if strong and courageous, may earn a higher position on the social ladder.

These red-faced Japanese macaques live in groups of about 200.

SWINGING BABIES

As mammals, the babies of apes and monkeys survive on their mother's milk. For warmth and protection, they cling to their mother until they are big enough to move about on their own.

AMAZON ▶ TWINS

Most monkeys and apes give birth to a single infant. The marmosets of the Amazon are one of the few exceptions. They usually have twins.

HANG TIGHT ▲

Apes and monkeys are always on the move, and there's no time to stop for a struggling infant. Mothers go about their regular business—climbing, hanging, leaping from one limb to another—all with baby on board.

SHOW OF COLOR

Babies need special care. One way to get it is to look really different from the adults—by being bright orange! In contrast to its gray relatives, this colorful silver leaf monkey seems to "scream" for everyone's attention. But in adulthood it, too, will grow gray fur.

94

PLAYTIME

Playing games and goofing off is as much fun for young apes and monkeys as it is for you. During play, youngsters make friendships that can last throughout their life. Playing also helps young monkeys learn the rules of the group.

▼ Wrestling on a limb develops the muscles and reflexes of these two young Japanese macaques.

For a young proboscis monkey, playing with a fat tail is just as much fun as climbing a tree.

ALL GROWN UP ▲

Male mountain gorillas acquire the silver hair on their back around age 10. At this point they must leave the group. They may live alone for a while, but will gradually find female gorillas from other groups to join them and help start their own troop.

TAKING CARE

Many monkey and ape dads protect their family. But caring for babies often falls to the female. Among langurs, females gather around a new baby, as if asking the mother for a chance to hold it. The mother lets them, but if danger approaches, she grabs the baby and dashes up a tree.

FUNKY MONKEYS

What does it take to set a monkey apart from the others? Maybe an extraordinary nose or a colorful face? If so, these monkeys take the prize.

LONG LEGS ▼
Reaching speeds of 35 miles per hour, the patas monkey is the fastest around, and long legs are part of its secret. Because it stays mostly on the ground, ranging the plains of Africa with hyenas and leopards, its speed is a much needed defense.

◄ BIG-EYED
The night monkey, with its very large round eyes, is the only monkey in the world that is *nocturnal,* or active at night. Found in Central and South America, night monkeys feed on fruit and leaves, and sleep in hollow trees during the day. Not surprisingly, they are also called owl monkeys.

BATHING BEAUTIES
Monkeys taking a bath? Not exactly. In the cold, snowy mountains of Japan, these macaques sit in hot springs just to get warm.

NOSEY GUY

With his large fleshy nose, the male *proboscis* (meaning nose) monkey got his name fair and square. These monkeys are found only on the island of Borneo, Malaysia, where they live in swamp forests and along creeks near the sea. They are good swimmers, and can even swim underwater.

◀ LIP FLIP

Geladas are large monkeys with a patch of naked, pink skin on their chest. These baboons have a strange-looking way of baring their teeth and gums. They flip back their lip!

COLOR COUNTS ▼

A male mandrill has bright blue cheeks and a red nose, which brightens when he is challenged. If that isn't enough to discourage outsiders, he has very sharp canines, four inches long!

◀ BLUSHER

The uakari (wah-CAR-ee), has a red face and bald head! It's an amazingly expressive monkey. When really angry or excited, its face turns even brighter. If it feels threatened, it shakes the branches and makes a noise that sounds like laughter.

INCREDIBLE CHIMPS

Chimps are so inventive, they'
been known to make their ow
"shoes"—using twigs as sanda
to protect their feet from thorr
They also use rocks to crack op
nuts, eat bitter plants to cu
stomachaches, a
hunt in organiz
group

ALL SIZED UP

Stand next to a common adult male chimp and you'll find he's not very small. He may reach 5 feet in height and weigh as much as 170 pounds. A second species, known as bonobos, are almost the same size. They live in the rain forests of Zaire, whereas the common chimp ranges the forests and savannas of western and central Africa.

HAN
ON, KI

Gettir
around mea
hanging on to mothe
Baby chimps cling
their mother as soon
they're born and sta
close to her for abo
five year
Wherever sh
goes, the bal
chimp is aboar
for the rid

HAT A HOOT

With up to 120 members living in eir group, chimps ve to communi- e. When they find od, they hoot, eam, and slap s. Even young mps can make as ny as 32 ferent unds.

REAL PERSONALITY

Can you tell one chimp from another? Next time you go to the zoo, spend some time with these primates. Their face, voice, walk, and personality are so different from one another that it takes primatologists just a few days to easily distinguish 20 or more chimps.

EXPRESS YOURSELF

On seeing a waterfall, one group of chimpanzees performed a dance, as if awed by the water. Chimps say a lot with their body, especially their face. They pout when they surrender to an attacker, and grin when excited or afraid. They can also look thoughtful or disbelieving.

BIG DIET

At one time, people thought chimps were strictly plant eaters. But primatologist Jane Goodall discovered that chimps on occasion also eat meat, such as monkeys, pigs, birds, and antelopes. They may eat a quarter-pound of meat in one day when hunting.

FIERCE FIGHTS

Ve usually think of chimpanzees as fun-loving and silly. t fights among male chimps over leadership can result serious injuries. In one population, neighboring bands chimpanzees were even observed waging deadly war.

This young chimp has only fun in mind! ▶

ORANGUTANS

Found only in portions of Borneo and Sumatra, this reddish-brown ape is known as the orangutan, or "person of the forest." The name suits it because an orangutan hardly ever comes out of the trees, living as much as 100 feet above the forest floor.

FRUIT LOVERS

The orangutan, who spends more than half the day eating, is the largest fruit-eating animal in the world. In the tropical forests, different kinds of fruit become ripe at different times of the year. The orangutan eats figs, mangoes, and its favorite fruit—the large, prickly durian. When fruit can't be found, the orangutan dines on leaves and bark.

NOTABLE LIP

Orangutan lips come in handy whe both hands and feet are needed t travel. Opened wide, they can hold large piece of fruit. Orangutans also us their lips to feel the fruit, puckering up an touching them to the surface

SHOUT IT OUT

A male orangutan's territory is about two square miles, and he shouts a clear warning to protect it. His morning "long call" is a series of roars and groans that can go on for nearly five minutes. Even in the dense growth of the rain forest, the call is heard by other orangutans as far as a mile away.

WILD LOOKS

Orangutans have some pretty wild looks—with arms one and a half times longer than their legs. And they are not so small. The males are about 5 feet tall and 220 pounds. The females are about half as heavy.

◄ With age, the male orangutan develops large cheek and chest pouches which frame his face.

ESCAPE ARTIST

There is no doubt that orangutans are smart. In zoos, they're known as escape artists. An orangutan named Bob broke out of three different cages at the San Diego Zoo, including one that had successfully held lions and grizzly bears.

LONERS

The orangutan is the most unsociable of all apes and monkeys. Male orangutans are loners. After mating with a female, they return to their solitary life. Mothers will sometimes feed and travel with other females and their young, but only for a short time. Baby orangutans stay with their mom for about six years.

ACROBATIC

Orangutans are great acrobats. Their strong arms, which span eight feet, really get them around. They prefer to travel by swinging rather than come down from their tree and walk. In fact, down on the ground orangutans are quite clumsy.

THE GREATEST APE

When early European explorers came back from Africa, they told fantastic stories about the gorilla's enormous size and savage temper. African gorillas are huge, but they are also very shy and peaceful. Their only natural enemies are people.

LAID BACK

Gorillas take it easy. They only travel about 400 yards per day. The group get up at dawn to begin feeding, then move into their nest of leaves and grasses for the afternoon, where adults relax and groom, and youngsters play. In late afternoon they rise to feed again, but by sunset are back in their nest for the night.

SHOW OFF ▼

When two gorilla groups meet, things can be tense. The dominant male silverbacks may put on elaborate, lengthy displays to intimidate one another—glaring, hooting, chest-beating, and standing on two legs. Each leader is concerned about protecting his troop.

THE BOSS

It's an awesome sight when a male silverback stands upright and begins hooting and chest-beating. His actions mean different things depending on the situation. He may be warning his group of danger or telling a male intruder he is not welcome.

◀ A COOL DRINK

Gorillas feed heavily on succulent (water-holding) plants such as wild celery. Since these plants are so rich in water, gorillas seldom have need for drinking water in the wild. A thirsty gorilla can also usually find a leaf with rain or condensation on it, and lick off the water.

SMART TALKER ▼

Apes are great communicators. One famous gorilla named Koko, who lives at The Gorilla Foundation, has even learned to use more than 500 words in American Sign Language. For her twenty-fifth birthday, Koko asked for a box of "scary" rubber snakes and lizards!

▲ A female's closest relationships are with the silverback and her babies.

NOSE PRINTS

Like human fingerprints, each gorilla has a unique nose print—the lines above the nostrils. The flare or shape of a gorilla's nostrils are also unique. Researchers use these visual marks to identify each gorilla in a group.

TO THE RESCUE

Apes and monkeys are quickly disappearing as forests and grasslands are cleared for farms, houses, and roads. More than 50 percent of these and other primates are considered endangered at this time. But many people are working very hard to save them.

ZOO DUTY ▲

Through breeding and reintroduction programs, zoos are helping endangered apes and monkeys. Young golden lion tamarins born in zoos are taught how to find food and live in the wild. Eventually they are released back into their South American home.

▼ The endangered cotton-top tamarin is being bred in zoos.

In the eyes of a caged chimp, there is only sadness.

AWAY WITH CAGES

Zoos have made a tremendous effort to create living conditions very similar to an animal's natural habitat. So if you visit a zoo, you probably will not see apes and monkeys in cages. They have trees to climb, vines on which to swing, and grassy areas where they can play.

APE HERO

Might the peaceful, intelligent gorilla have compassion for human life? Think of the gorilla Binti. In 1996, she rescued a three-year-old boy who fell 18 feet into the gorilla exhibit at Brookfield Zoo in Illinois. She picked the boy up, cradled him, then carried him to the zookeepers' door.

Some monkeys can adapt to major changes in their habitat. In Costa Rica, after its forest habitat was cleared for farming, the white-faced capuchin monkey learned to travel on fences instead of trees, and switched to eating food found in cattle pastures and fruit plantations.

GOOD GOODALL ▶

For decades, Jane Goodall studied chimps in the wild. But her work did not stop when she left the field. She set up sanctuaries for orphaned chimps, persuaded scientists to improve conditions for the chimps used in medical research, and began speaking to people about habitat loss in Africa.

LIFE'S WORK

Mountain gorillas received life-saving assistance from researcher Dian Fossey, who lived among these apes from 1963 to 1985. Besides gathering remarkable information, she saved them from extinction by chasing off poachers and making the world aware of gorilla endangerment.

At the edge of the shrinking forest, these gorillas investigate a farmer's expanding field.

Index

Glossary

pha Male: Leader and most powerful member of a olf pack.

chiate: To swing from object to object, such as tree bs, using the arms.

che: Hole that dogs and wolves use for storing and rying food to eat at a later time.

mbium: Part of a tree that lies beneath the bark; ars eat cambium.

mouflage: Way that an animal disguises and protects elf by appearing to blend into its surroundings.

nidae: Family that dogs and wolves belong to.

nine Teeth: Sharp, pointed teeth near the front of the outh used for tearing and shredding flesh; mammals ually have four canines.

rnassials: Teeth in the back of the mouth, also called olars, that are used for grinding and crushing.

rnivore: Animal that eats the flesh of other animals.

ld-blooded: Having a body temperature that is not gulated internally but adapts to the temperature of rounding air or water; reptiles and amphibians are ld-blooded.

n: Underground burrow where animals are born, e, and hibernate.

urnal: Animal that is active during the day.

minant: Aggressive animal usually considered the der of its family or group.

dangered: Species that is threatened with extinction.

olve: To gradually change and develop.

tinct: Animals and plants that have died out and no ger exist.

ines: Cats

od Chain: Series of living things in which each feeds on the one below it and in turn is eaten by the one ove it; cycle repeats itself until the tiniest animal eats e bacteria that is left behind from the largest animal.

oom: To make neat by cleaning or brushing.

Habitat: Natural surroundings of a particular animal.

Herbivore: Animal that eats only fruits, plants, and vegetables.

Hibernate: To rest, or sleep, and remain inactive through the winter; animals that hibernate survive on the food stored in their bodies until spring.

Marsupial: Mammal that carries its babies in a pouch, such as a kangaroo and koala.

Nocturnal: Animal that is active during the night.

Omega: Lowest-ranking member of a wolf pack that is often picked on by the rest of the pack.

Omnivore: Animal that eats plants and animals; most bears and primates are omnivores.

Pack: Group, or family, of dogs or wolves.

Playfighting: Way that animals develop strength and hunting skills, by fighting playfully with others.

Poacher: Someone who hunts or steals unlawfully.

Predator: Animal that hunts other animals for food.

Preserve: Large tract of land, set aside by law, for animals to live on.

Prey: An animal that is hunted by other animals for food.

Pride: Group, or family, of lions.

Primate: Mammal group that includes humans, apes, and monkeys.

Primatologist: Scientist who studies primates.

Proboscis: Long, flexible nose of a mammal.

Species: Group of similar organisms that can produce offspring with one another.

Stalk: To hunt slowly and quietly.

Submissive: Lower-ranking member of an animal family or group.

Vertebrae: Small bones that make up the backbone.

Warm-blooded: Having a high body temperature that is regulated internally and is not affected by surroundings; birds and mammals are warm-blooded.